WHAT IS REIKI MAGIC?

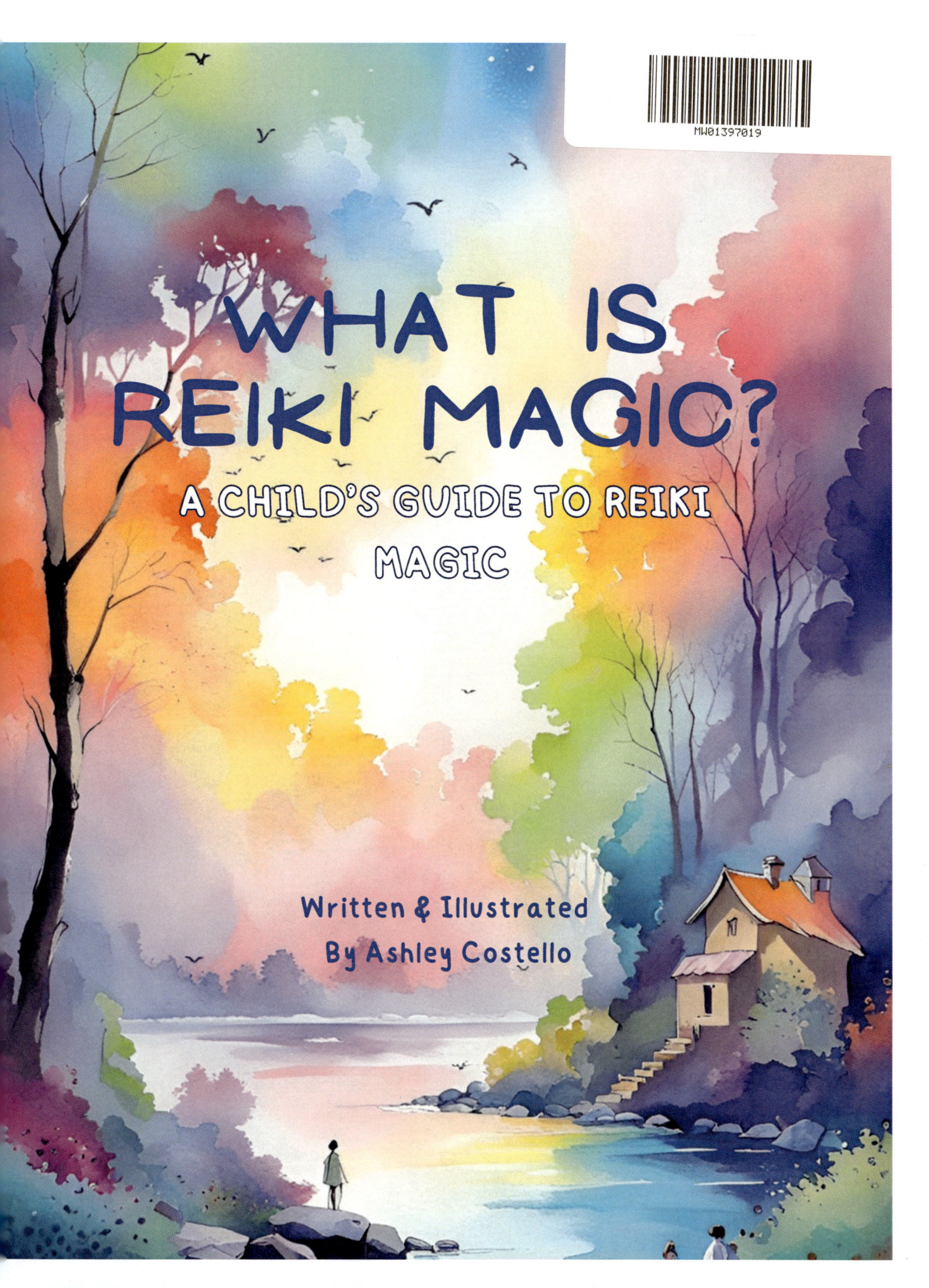

A CHILD'S GUIDE TO REIKI MAGIC

Written & Illustrated

By Ashley Costello

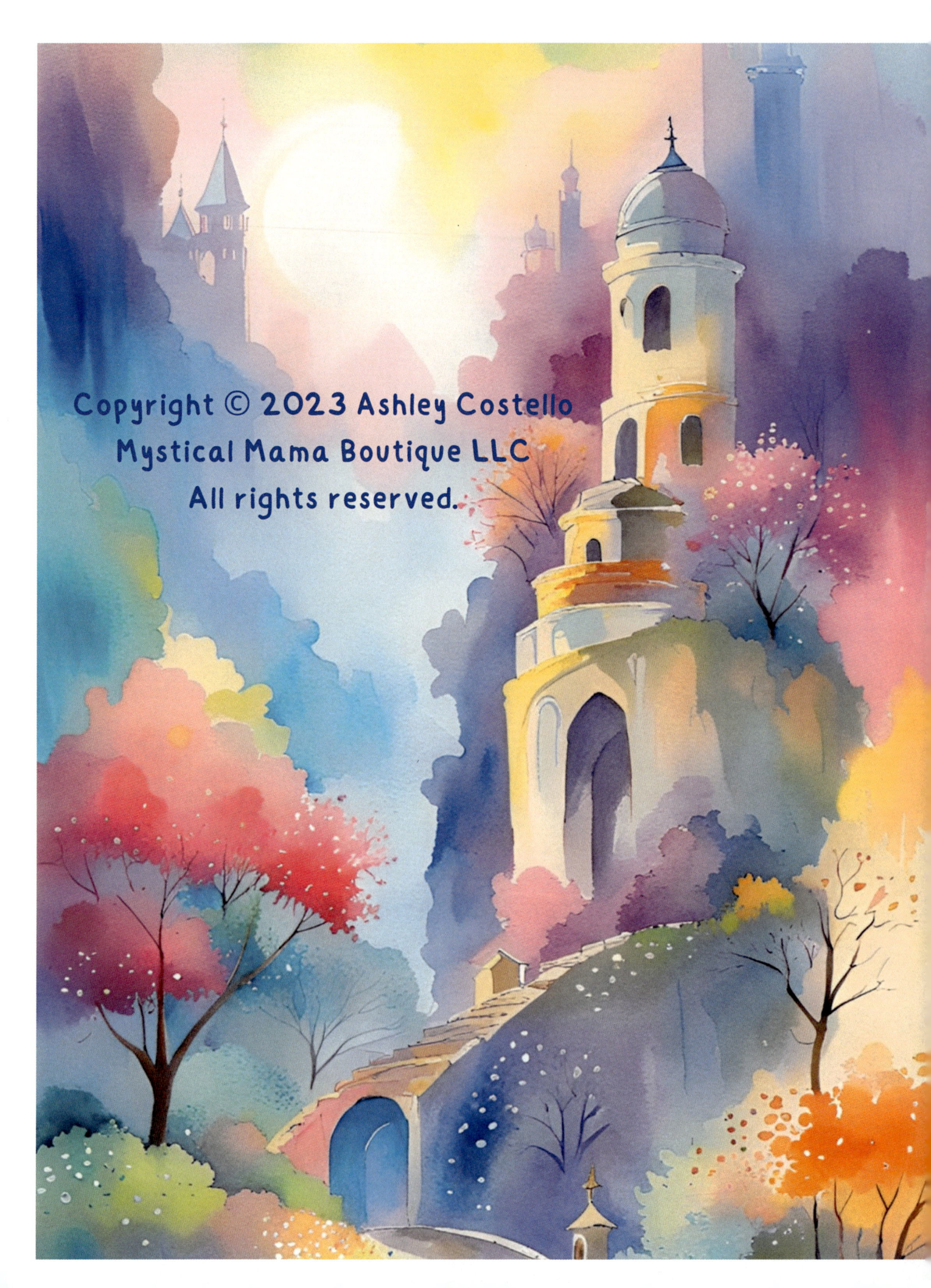

Copyright © 2023 Ashley Costello
Mystical Mama Boutique LLC
All rights reserved.

DEDICATION

To my sun,
my moon,
& all my stars
I love you
Sly

NOTE TO PARENTS

Dear Parents,

I wanted to take a moment to provide some context about the book you are about to read with your child, which introduces the topic of Reiki. Reiki is a form of energy healing that focuses on promoting balance and well-being.

In this book, the concept of Reiki is presented in a child-friendly and accessible manner. It aims to introduce children to the idea that they have the power to promote their own healing and happiness.

It's important to note that Reiki is a complementary therapy, meaning it is not a substitute for traditional medical care. While it can be a wonderful tool for relaxation, self-care, and promoting a sense of calm, it's essential to continue seeking professional medical advice when needed.

As you read this book with your child, you may want to engage in discussions about the power of positive intention, the importance of self-care, and the connection between the mind, body, and emotions. Encourage your child to ask questions and explore their own understanding of healing and well-being.

Remember, this book is intended to serve as an introduction to Reiki and promote curiosity and open-mindedness. It's always a good idea to encourage children to explore various perspectives and approaches to well-being while emphasizing the importance of maintaining a balanced and informed view.

Enjoy your reading journey with your child, and may it spark meaningful conversations and a deeper appreciation for the wonders of healing and self-care.

In health,
Ashley Costello

WHAT IS REIKI MAGIC?
A CHILD'S GUIDE TO REIKI MAGIC

Written & Illustrated
By Ashley Costello

Reiki Magic is Mama, kissing my boo boos.

Reiki Magic is Dada, giving me a bear hug.

Reiki Magic is the healing love from snuggling my dog.

Reiki Magic is sharing my favorite book.

Reiki Magic is playing with my friends.

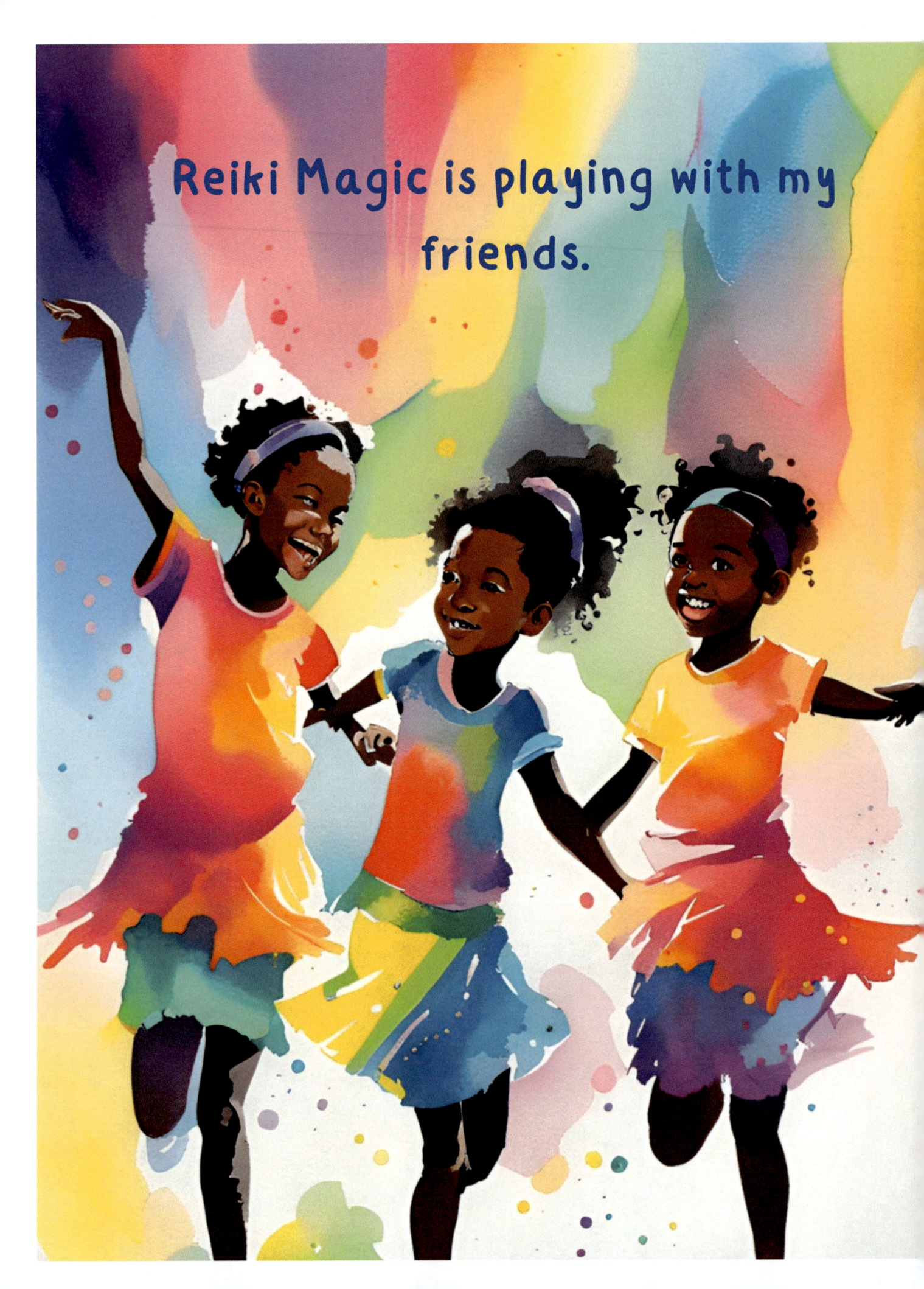

Reiki Magic is jumping in my bed.

Reiki Magic is baked into all of Granny's cookies.

Reiki Magic is water splashing in my tub.

Reiki Magic is my teacher expanding my horizons.

Reiki Magic is a helping hand held out to give us guidance.

Reiki Magic is the sea and the skies.

Reiki Magic is watching fireflies.

Reiki Magic is catching snowflakes on my tongue.

Reiki Magic is the safe feeling when I'm wrapped in my blanky.

Reiki Magic is the stars glistening in the skies above.

Reiki Magic is getting tucked into bed with love.

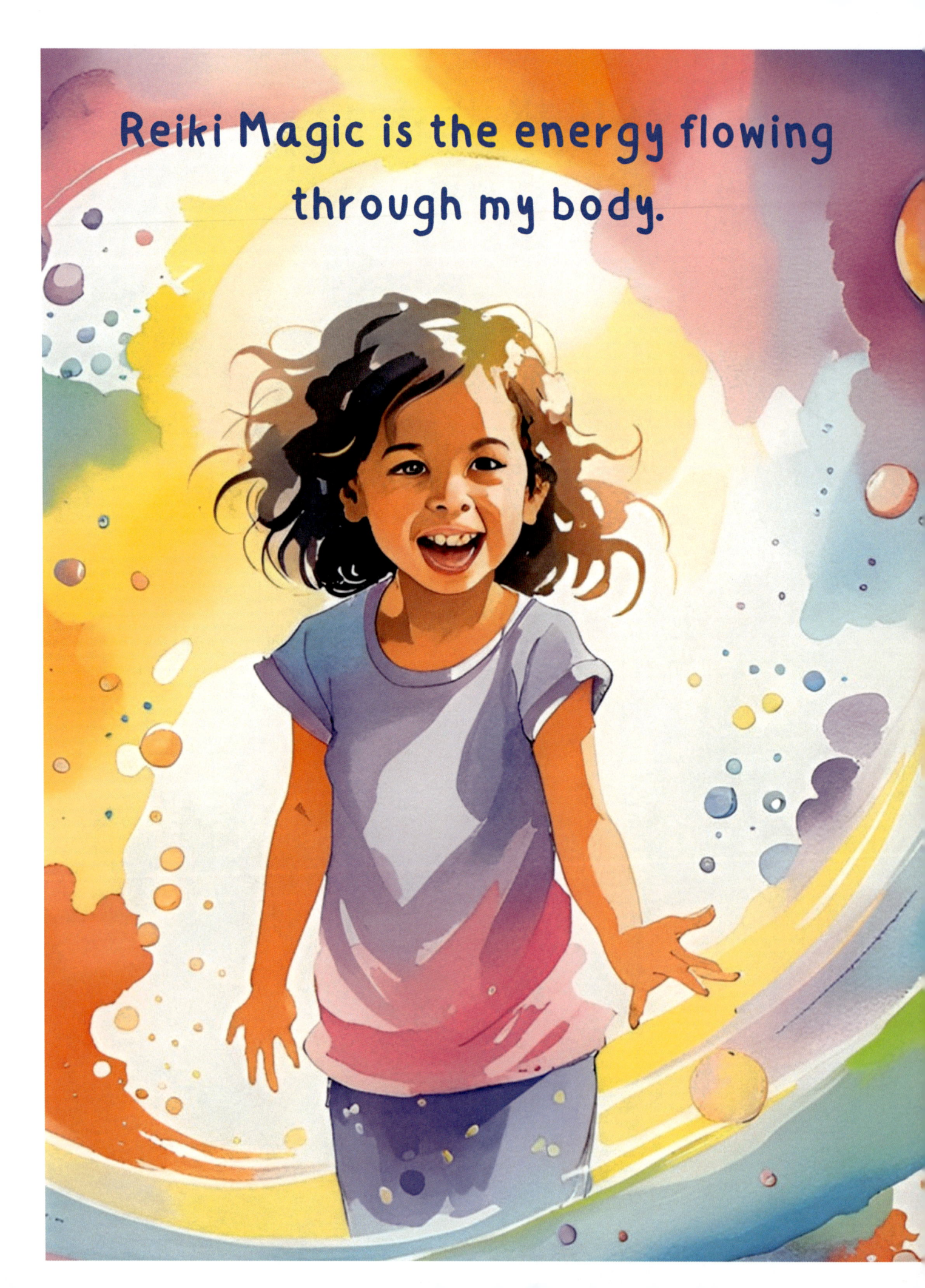

Reiki Magic is the energy flowing through my body.

Reiki Magic is what gets my Aura shining.

Reiki Magic is the superpower inside me and you.

Reiki Magic is saying
I love you!

THE END

ACKNOWLEDGEMENTS

Andrew & Sly, thank you for being my reason why.
Mom & Kaylee, thank you for always believing me.
Ricky, Jorge & Alonso, thank for always inspiring me.
Janel Ann Manente, @SpiritualGirlYoga thank you for introducing me to Reiki.

Truly Grateful for you.

IN LOVING MEMORY OF
Roxxii

April 2009 - August 2023

In Love & Light

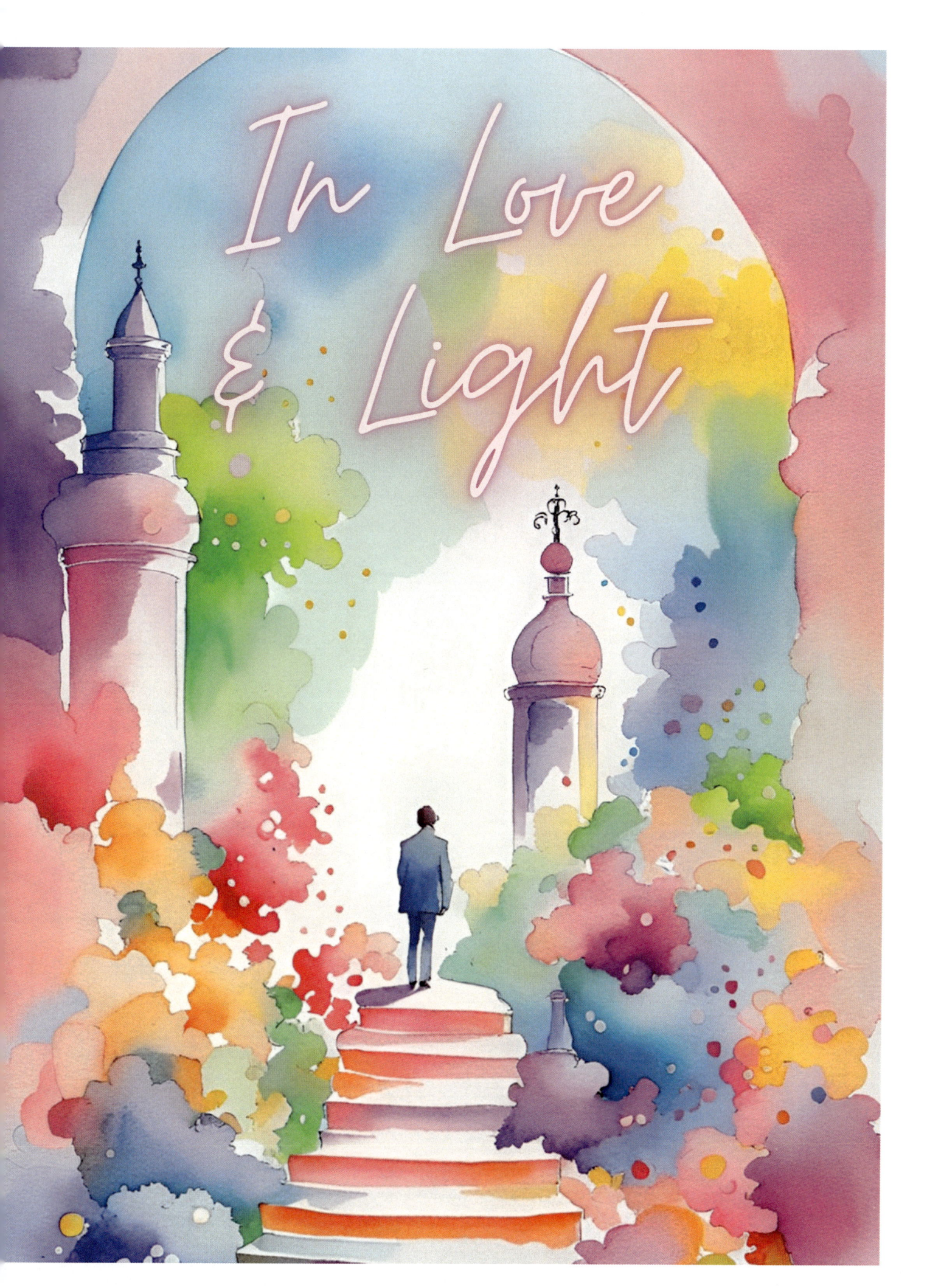

Reiki Magic: A Journey of Love & Light
Coming Winter 2023

FOLLOW US FOR EXCLUSIVE CONTENT

www. MysticalMamaBoutique.com

@MysticalMamaBoutique

ABOUT THE AUTHOR

Ashley Costello is an accomplished Reiki Master Practitioner & author who delves into the realms of spirituality, self-discovery, and personal growth. With a keen understanding of the human experience, Ashley's writings offer profound insights and practical guidance to those seeking a deeper connection to themselves and the world around them.

Her words resonate with authenticity and wisdom, drawing from her own spiritual journey and experiences as a Reiki Master and owner of Mystical Mama Boutique. Through her writings, Ashley explores various topics such as energy healing, mindfulness, intuitive development, and the power of self-love.

Ashley's writing style is captivating, blending storytelling with thought-provoking concepts. Her ability to convey complex ideas in a relatable and accessible manner allows readers to engage with her work on a profound level. Each page is infused with her genuine desire to uplift and empower others, encouraging them to explore their inner landscapes and embrace their true potential.

Whether she is sharing practical techniques, providing insightful reflections, or offering heartfelt anecdotes, Ashley's writing carries a transformative energy that inspires readers to embark on their personal journeys of self-discovery and spiritual growth.

As an author, Ashley Costello's words have the power to ignite a spark within readers, encouraging them to embark on a path of self-exploration and embrace the wonders of the spiritual realm. Her contributions to the literary world leave a lasting impact, guiding individuals towards a deeper understanding of themselves and the universe they inhabit.

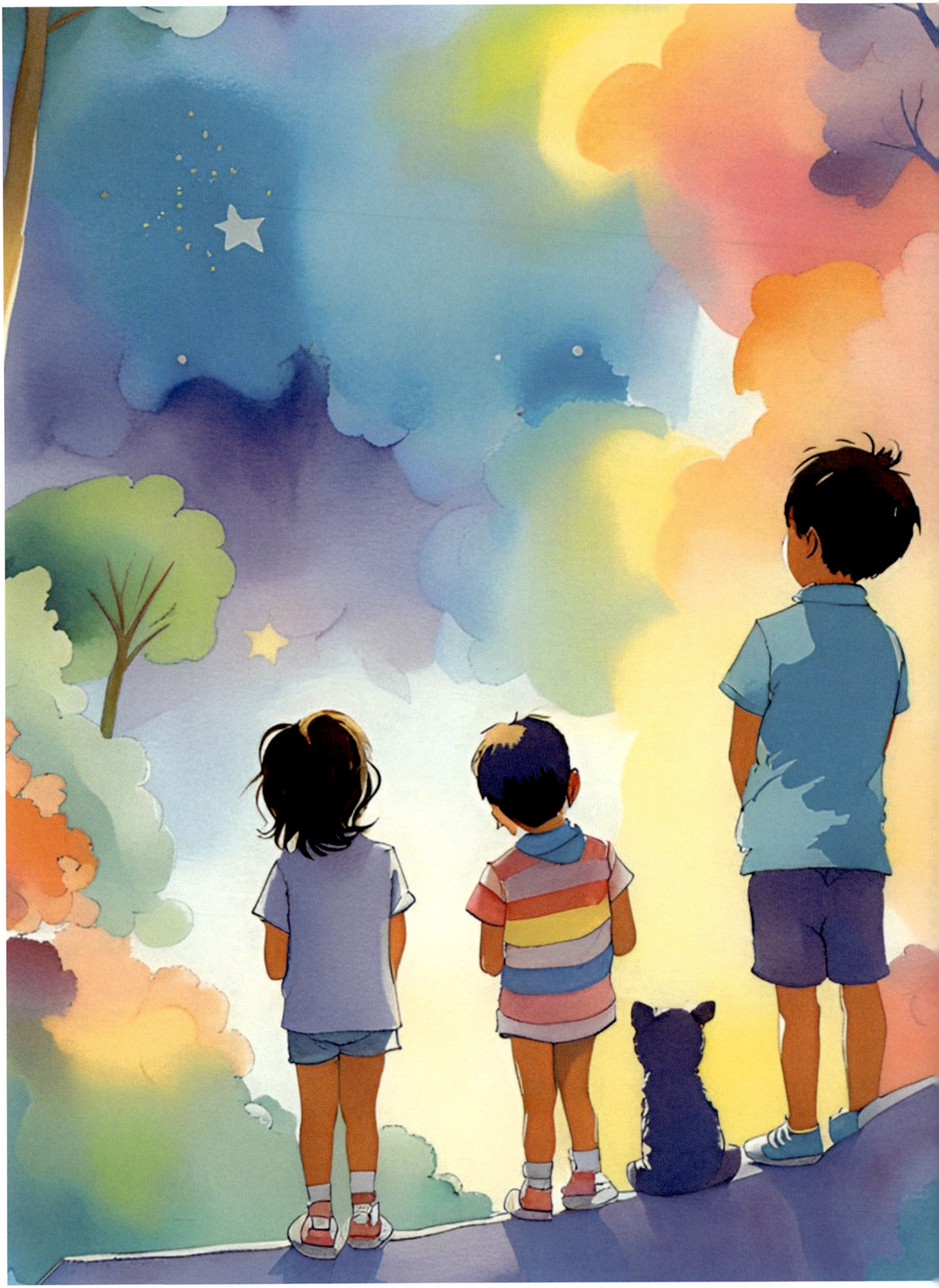